PRAISE FOR JACQUELINE PIRTLE

"Jacqueline takes you always directly to what you are ready to see or experience."

— LONGTIME CLIENT AND READER

"It is liberating to face your own blocks and to be finally free of the weight that they have caused for many years. And while for me the changes I'm experiencing are noticeable and real, I still feel like myself. Just a more sure self."

— LONGTIME CLIENT AND READER

"Jacqueline makes me BELIEVE I can be and live a joyful and magical existence every new day of my life!"

— LONGTIME CLIENT AND READER

JACQUELINE PIRTLE

Align, Expand, and Calibrate!

Your Stairway to Joy

A 30 day journal

COPYRIGHT

Copyright © 2021 Jacqueline Pirtle
www.FreakyHealer.com

All rights reserved. No part of this book may be reproduced or transmitted in any form or by any means, electronic or mechanical, including photocopying, recording, or by any information storage and retrieval system without the written permission of the publisher, except where permitted by law.

ISBN-13: 978-1-955059-27-5

Publisher: Freaky Healer

Editor-in-chief: Zoe Pirtle
All-round Support: Mitch Pirtle

Book cover design by Kingwood Creations kingwoodcreations.com

Author photo courtesy of Lionel Madiou madious.com

I want to let you know that all my books and work as a holistic practitioner are a wholesome system, supporting you to live a more conscious, mindful, and happier life.

However, I made it so you can receive the benefit of living more joyously solely by working through this terrific journal book, while also experiencing the full satisfaction in continuing on to the next journal of this series—not to mention the rock solid tools you get by reading any of my other books or adding in my podcast *The Daily Freak*. Either way, I know you'll love my inspirational teachings.

Find out more at:
FreakyHealer.com
Amazon - Jacqueline Pirtle's Author Page
The Daily Freak Podcast

Before you dive in, I want to thank you for hopping on the magic train with me! I truly hope you enjoy **Align, Expand, and Calibrate** as much as I loved writing it, and if you do, it would be wonderful if you could take a short minute and leave a review on Amazon and Goodreads.com as soon as you can.

Your kind feedback helps other readers find my books more easily, and to be happy faster. Consider it a joy-deed for the world.

Thank you!

ACKNOWLEDGMENTS

Let's be honest here… I have a dream team!

I could not have finished this book without the help of talented, creative, high-for-life, and phenomenal professionals.

From the bottom of my heart, I want to thank Zoe Pirtle for her editorial mastery; Mitch Pirtle for his all-round support; kingwoodcreations.com for their fun and polished book cover design; and madiouART.com for an amazing photo shoot.

I'd also like to extend a huge "Thank You!" to all fans of my work and books—I created this beautiful journal series for you.

Life is spectacular with you on my side!

***Align** yourself with who you really are.*
***Expand** that aligned YOU.*
***Calibrate** into your new height!*

DEDICATION

I dedicate this journal to anyone who feels blahhh - emotionally, physically, or energetically - and with all my might, will pull them into their alignment, expansion, and calibration.

INTRODUCTION

Lovable YOU,

It is, indeed, an intense time that brings forth the values we actually treasure, while also highlighting new ways that keep us going in the long run—or at least until we are shown an even newer version of different. But either way, you are here now, so I hope that you believe in your long-haul.

My heart is filled to the brim to be able to share with you how you can validate your longevity and dive deep into the essence of who you really are, immerse yourself there, and live from that substance filled with energy, wisdom, beauty, and life—becoming unquestionably clear that you are in charge of how - and also what - your quality of existence is and that you can change yourself to being and living more aligned, expanded, and calibrated at any time you wish!

Let's face it:

Without alignment with your deepest inner truth of who you really are, it's easy to feel lost and life can be uncertain. You are missing out on the beauty that you are and what life could be for you.

Without expansion, you are not able to show up as the bigness

INTRODUCTION

that you naturally are—however, if not aligned first, expansion can get you into the direction of unwell-feeling.

Without calibration, you are not being and living the high-for-life energy you came here to BE. But beware, calibrating without aligning only gets you feeling better until whatever - chocolate, cake, or ice cream for instance - that happy-fied you wears off; when calibrating while aligned keeps you shifting higher and higher since there is never a ceiling as to how amazing you can feel. Or take calibration with alignment but no expansion—the steam to get all the way up on your feeling ladder will be little, or missing.

You really, really, really are invited to use the whole system of aligning first, expanding second, and calibrating with joy into the infinite and beyond in order to truly BE and live YOU. I cannot press this point enough!

You might ask, "Is it hard?" No it is not, and anybody who tells you otherwise is wrong, because it's not like you need to learn something new—you already know how to do it and you already ARE all that bliss! All you need is knowledge, practice, and to choose, commit, and focus on a lifestyle that feels amazing—then cultivate it to make it your normal way of existing. Think of it like you are going to the beach in a full body-armor-suit but realize on the spot that it is not fitting or comfortable, so right then and there you plan on wearing a bathing suit next time you go beaching and commit to focus on remembering that more aligned choice you just made—the outcome being that when the day comes and you head to the beach in your bathing suit, you will feel amazing, so much so that you will always put this new custom as a priority since you are now hooked on how incredible it feels.

Alignment, expansion, and calibration shoots you into the sky with the stars; and there - in that open space - a whole world of possibilities, wellness, happiness, and wonder awaits—as well as limitless wisdom that comes from your energetic part - your soul

INTRODUCTION

being, your inner you, your higher self, or however you wish to call it - but also from your one-ness with consciousness, where all information is held.

You are a whole being comprised of a physical body, mind, soul, and consciousness, here to experience life through physicality and alignment with your soul being—expanding and calibrating into *bigger* and *more* at all times through human-ness and from the core of the energetic essence that makes everything and everyone. As part of that energetic bundle, you are vibrating in frequencies, some lower than others—preferably higher ones, since they are the frequencies that feel truly amazing. You are capable of switching between these frequencies as you wish. Simply said, what you focus on is how you feel and how you feel creates your next—it's like you are holding a compass and can constantly see where you are, but also where you are headed to:

- I am aligned—feeling great
- I am aligned and expanded—feeling great and powerful
- I am aligned, expanded, and calibrated—feeling great, powerful, and over the moon blissful
- Unaligned, not expanded, not calibrated—without a clue, unwell, and can't stay happy to save your life

This ***Align, Expand, and Calibrate*** journal exists to help you to BE and live more of YOU and grab this time of intensity with your heart—to shift to feeling amazing anyways, no matter what, by helping you to turn your old ways upside down - and inside out - so the old unconnected way doesn't exist anymore. From there you can find new and unique preferences that fit your aligned being, so you will go out into the world being the bright light that you actually are.

I say, let's not lose another second to any unaligned misery; and instead - as your new aligned, expanded, and calibrated YOU - create a life beyond your dreams where an ocean of opportuni-

INTRODUCTION

ties will catch hold of you, not to mention you will become ONE with joy and gain the excitement of living an extraordinary life filled with incredible manifestations

Surely you understand that such a lifestyle still includes ups and downs, lefts and rights—lots of great moments for you to practice aligning, expanding, and calibrating. Being okay with however things are - even in hard times - and creating pure alignment by not giving any unaligned thing the oxygen to be the main attraction in your life, means that you are making your aligned, expanded, and calibrated YOU the main star. Just consider the epic-ness of that!

Journaling through this 30 day edition of *Align, Expand, and Calibrate* gives your best version of you the spotlight and brings a huge heightening into the equation so you can experience life like you never have before, craft a time beyond your expectations, and love what you live—to the extent of becoming a master in living consciously, mindfully, and feeling phenomenal, while manifesting the best of the best. It's a change that is forever!

As a side note, there are a couple of bonus days at the end in case you ever find the need to do two entries in a day, or so you can keep working while you wait for the next journal in this series to arrive. I also left you a few blank *Align, Expand, and Calibrate* pages to journal about deepening your ways of being proudly alive.

Enough chit-chat, I know you are ready—so grab your pen and have incredible fun catching more life than you have ever caught in your new crazy ways.

Happiest,
    Jacqueline

 ay 1

IMAGINE the most magical and beautiful stairway, one of light and pureness—made of glass, wood, earth, or whatever material is most heart-touching for you. Make this your stairway to joy! Then, visualize your flight of stairs going high up into a space of the infinite, beautiful, and bright nothingness - into consciousness - with the last step meeting the heavens. Sit with this image, stare at it, laugh and cry with it—while filling yourself with its essence of love, light, and holiness. How does this feel for you?

Every split second in life you get to choose to run up those stairs and live in that essence of pure positive energy, or to stay where you are in physicality while only living from that limited space—with yet another option being to only take a few steps up and live half way.

Just think about it—creatively, uniquely, and playfully rushing up your stairway to ecstasy, with every step getting you happier and more inspired to BE and live YOU.

Now that you have created your visionary path of enlightenment we can get into the rootedness of how you take your first step, then - while being endlessly fueled and energized - run up without ever stopping. So be excited—the teachings of alignment, expansion, and calibration are splashed across the next few pages.

_____
_____
_____

Align, Expand, and Calibrate - Your Stairway to Joy

 ay 2

TIME TO FUEL up and energize—time to align!

You are at the bottom of your magical stairway to joy, looking up with excitement and an "I can't wait" attitude, ready to take your first step but also eager to get rushing—for which you need unlimited and powerful fuel that carries you, without any doubt, up and into this infinite field of consciousness.

That is where the alignment with your inner being - your soul being, your higher self, the Divine, or however you would like to call it - comes into the picture because your inner you is pure positive energy, always knows what's best for you, and is the most rock-solid guidance to your bliss; aside from being your immediate and innate connection to the field of consciousness that you are always ONE with. Naturally, aligning with your inner voice will guide you up your stairway while fueling you all the way.

I say, close your eyes and breathe into this purifying fact. Let yourself float around in your nothingness to find your alignment with your everything-ness—your inner you. There, ask yourself, "What is alignment for me, what guidance am I getting, and how does my alignment feel?"

Time to align, align, and align some more!

___

___

___

___

Align, Expand, and Calibrate - Your Stairway to Joy

 ay 3

TODAY WE EXPAND. Like a ballon, but don't worry—you will never ever pop since there is no limit to how much you can expand into being you. No limit; just think about that!

Latching onto yesterday's wisdom of aligning with who you really are - a well-feeling energetic being here to experience physical life - it's time to get bigger as that ecstatic YOU.

Imagine your grandness - your pure positive energy - getting bigger, bigger, and bigger—filling every single cell of yours, then growing beyond yourself, even bigger and bigger, until you are flowing into the outer-world and even there getting bigger and bigger to reach beyond and all the way into the infinite.

You are expanding your wholesome YOU; your aligned power, knowledge, connectedness, and incredibly bright light to BE and live as ONE with, in, and through the nothingness of the Universe.

How does that feel—to BE and live that aligned and expanded YOU?

_____
_____
_____
_____
_____
_____
_____
_____
_____

Align, Expand, and Calibrate - Your Stairway to Joy

 ay 4

CALIBRATE YOURSELF INTO A HIGHER, purer, and brighter essence to BE and live as the highest YOU in the most heightened event of all time—your life!

Why? Because for one, you can, and two, how else could you possibly want to live aside from experiencing the whole life-show fully? Lastly, three: life and you are an ongoing development, so keep up with that skyrocketing way of being because there is never a ceiling to how calibrated you can feel.

It's like you are climbing your stairway to joy, bliss, happiness, health, success, abundance, and all that you want to BE and have —always higher and higher while never stopping or going back down, knowing that higher and purer is your calling and that living life is an opportunity to immerse yourself into more and more well feeling.

How does this feel—what are your thoughts here? How will you take that next step to calibrate yourself into your new height?

_____
_____
_____
_____
_____
_____
_____
_____

Align, Expand, and Calibrate - Your Stairway to Joy

 ay 5

QUESTIONS OF THE DAY:
Are you aligned? Are you expanded? Are you calibrated—and do you keep aligning, expanding, and calibrating? Are you aligned with who you really are? Are you expanded as such? Are you calibrated into whatever life is for you right now?

Sit for a minute, close your eyes, and breathe into your inner space—potentize yourself! From there, imagine and sense yourself taking these uplifting steps and ascending your magical stairway.

How do you feel? How does everything look in this new height—how does it smell and taste up there, what new thoughts do you have?

Embrace your new day by being and living in that higher essence that you are, and constantly moving into. Wow, what an elevation—be prepared, wonder awaits!

_____
_____
_____
_____
_____
_____
_____
_____
_____
_____
_____
_____

Align, Expand, and Calibrate - Your Stairway to Joy

 Day 6

Issues, problems, drama, trouble, difficulties, hardships, and all other unwanted things that life readily offers at times are normal and not there for us to hate, or to wish they would disappear—instead, they exist to be embraced and for you to align with, expand in, and calibrate yourself to new plateaus where change is possible. So be OK with what IS, lean into everything, align with what it means, expand as that wiser you, and calibrate upward; taking the next steps on your stairway of bliss. Remember, your flight of stairs is always there and ready—no matter the circumstances.

What in your life is such a grand event that it just does not move or shift, despite your hard work? How can you align, expand, and calibrate in it?

Align, Expand, and Calibrate - Your Stairway to Joy

Day 7

YESTERDAY WE COVERED the unwanted that you can't change—today we tap into the unwanted that is, in fact, changeable by you.

What is in your life that you don't like, but could shift with a little more positiveness, a drop of joy, some laughter, or more play? Where could showing up as a more aligned, expanded, and calibrated YOU fit the bill? Where could you give a lot less momentum to the unwanted, and instead, focus straightforward on what you like or the outcome that you are wishing for?

_____
_____
_____
_____
_____
_____
_____
_____
_____
_____
_____
_____
_____
_____
_____
_____
_____

Align, Expand, and Calibrate - Your Stairway to Joy

 ay 8

WHEN YOU ENJOY something - be it food, music, or anything really - it means that you are aligned, not just with your inner being but also with what you are enjoying. That's double the win! What in your new day will you make sure to enjoy more consciously? How will you focus on the many alignments in that satisfaction—and how can you make more of this sweetness come to fruition?

_____
_____
_____
_____
_____
_____
_____
_____
_____
_____
_____
_____
_____
_____
_____
_____
_____

Align, Expand, and Calibrate - Your Stairway to Joy

 Day 9

YOU CHANGE—PHYSICALITY always changes, and life is constantly new and different with every split second there is. That's just how it works. Naturally, that brings into the equation the fact that your alignment with your inner you and who you really are is also of a changing nature—hence yesterday *this* felt great, but today something else would feel better. What an excitement that brings! You want to move with that thrill so keep yourself on your tippy toes and stay alert by aligning with this always-newness of yourself and life at all times. What is not feeling good for you right now—and what new alignment is possible?

Align, Expand, and Calibrate - Your Stairway to Joy

# Day 10

CLOSE YOUR EYES and take a nice big breath in while sensing yourself - energetically and physically - expanding more and more. Then, while breathing out, settle your expanded YOU by imagining yourself grounding deep down into Mother Earth—drilling yourself in a rooted matter into her core of love and nourishment. Again, breathe in and expand, and keep drilling while breathing out. Do this visualization, this sensing, for as long as you like and on you go into your new day—expanded and substantially powerful, as being the energy that you really are. Wow!

_____
_____
_____
_____
_____
_____
_____
_____
_____
_____
_____
_____
_____
_____

Align, Expand, and Calibrate - Your Stairway to Joy

# Day 11

ALIGNING IS like a superpower that is naturally always available for you to use and, once trained, you ARE - and stay - aligned without even focusing on it. But here's the catch; you can align with *this* or *that*, with what's good for you or what gets you into your personal abyss—maybe even someone else's "down" if you happen to latch onto theirs. So let's practice aligning with your bliss by focusing on what makes you feel amazing, all while noticing when you're aligning with the opposite. Are you feeling good right now and are you consciously aligning with that joy? Or are you not feeling good—and if so, what can you do about it?

Align, Expand, and Calibrate - Your Stairway to Joy

 ay 12

YESTERDAY WE SET the record straight for well-feeling and focused alignment, so let's add a little more to that…

Watchful, observant, and concentrated alignment means that you don't indulge in anything that is the opposite—no gossiping, no re-telling of the unwell, no sharing or wreaking havoc, and no feeding or nourishing anything that dims your light—or someone else's. How will you refrain from any of the above from now on?

Align, Expand, and Calibrate - Your Stairway to Joy

 ay 13

WHAT ALIGNED food are you dreaming of? Yes, there is such a thing as aligned food! How can you make this meal-magic happen? How will you expand in that enjoyment, calibrating into your highest joyful self while devouring the magic—maybe even sharing and spreading your bliss with a loud "Mmm..." or "Wow?" Can you include your loved ones in this delicious food-play?

Align, Expand, and Calibrate - Your Stairway to Joy

 ay 14

SOME DAYS it's best to hang around like a sloth, slow and lazy in a happy fashion. At other times, it is best to be a dolphin—playful, swift, and adventurous while moving powerfully and with the flow. There is also the feel of being a giraffe—seeing and experiencing everything from a birds-eye view. You change all the time, and so does your aligned physical activity level and way of being. What is best for you right now? Go on, keep up by aligning with your newness—one in which you can expand and calibrate to become a better feeling you.

Align, Expand, and Calibrate - Your Stairway to Joy

 ay 15

ALIGNMENT IS EVERYWHERE! The sidewalk shows you where to walk; how aligned! When driving, the lines show you how to stay in place—and in perfect alignment. Cooking with a recipe tells you all about alignment. When putting on pants, your legs give you the aligned direction. Alignment is all around you! Where can you notice it more, and how will you feel yourself - and expand and calibrate - into those great reminders?

Align, Expand, and Calibrate - Your Stairway to Joy

 ay 16

EXPANSION—YOU see it in hairbands, stretchy toys like *Monkey Noodles*, or any kind of dough—even play dough. Where in your surroundings do you notice expansion right now? Why not latch onto these possibilities of expansions that are, in truth, great invitations to feel yourself expanded at all times? Could getting yourself some stretchy slime be your constant reminder?

_____
_____
_____
_____
_____
_____
_____
_____
_____
_____
_____
_____
_____
_____
_____
_____
_____
_____
_____

Align, Expand, and Calibrate - Your Stairway to Joy

 ay 17

PHYSICAL EXPANSION IS JUST as important as energetic expansion. Stretching while doing exercise is a great way to practice and stay physically expanded, and since exercise is good for you, you are naturally aligned - that is, if you are enjoying your chosen fitness type - while also expanding in that wonderful alignment. Are you enjoying your physical activity—and if not, what's a good change? How will you move yourself into your well-feeling physical expansion more often and how can you make this widening count on your conscious level?

Align, Expand, and Calibrate - Your Stairway to Joy

 Day 18

ENERGETIC EXPANSION IS ACHIEVED by meditation, visualization, and imagination—then by sensing your energy as expanded. If you can tell the world to go away right now, do it, and get practicing to make this your normal and automatic way of being and living! If not, you can always set your expectation to "I AM expanded!" by breathing into the sensation of being wide, tall, stretching far, and by saying, thinking, or writing the words, "I AM always expanded!" Since this is just one of many mantra-ideas, what is the most fitting one that you can come up with; one that snaps you automatically into being the infinite energetic YOU that you naturally always ARE?

Align, Expand, and Calibrate - Your Stairway to Joy

 ay 19

THIS ONE IS EASY—COME up with your best ever mantra for snapping you out of your mis-alignment—and gets you with speed back into alignment? It could be as simple as, "I AM always aligned!" but I'm sure you can unique-fy that statement a thousand times more fitting for yourself. Go on, no holding back here, and keep returning to add more as you go!

Align, Expand, and Calibrate - Your Stairway to Joy

Day 20

ANOTHER MANTRA—ANOTHER chance of getting to know yourself better and better!

What is your shout-out for immediate calibration into the highest you that you are invited to BE and live? Keep this journal entry going - like a tab - by adding on while you live your beautiful life.

___

Align, Expand, and Calibrate - Your Stairway to Joy

 ay 21

EXPANSION ON A SOUL-LEVEL!

What does that look like for you? What insights does this bring—wisdom of more connectedness, being even more powerful and brighter than before; healthier, happier, or more abundance?

Your soul is always limitlessly expanded and invites you to play catch-up in every new split second that you are alive. How will you play the best ever gotcha-game with your inner YOU?

_____
_____
_____
_____
_____
_____
_____
_____
_____
_____
_____
_____
_____
_____
_____

Align, Expand, and Calibrate - Your Stairway to Joy

 ay 22

AN EXPANDED mind thinks expanded thoughts—musings like being open, allowing, receiving, and interested in new ways to experience life are of such a nature. How will you focus on expanding your mind more often? How will you let your old habits go and, instead, choose new exciting ones? Life is colorful, full of differences, and no one way is perfect. I say, give the unpredictable magic a go!

Align, Expand, and Calibrate - Your Stairway to Joy

 ay 23

CHALLENGE TIME!

Set a timer to give yourself a goal to get into alignment - like 5 minutes or so - then go do whatever it takes for you to feel connected and flowing with your inner being and well-feeling. Dance, breathe, smile, or juggle—see if you can succeed!

This helps you strengthen your joy-muscles to make your life the best it can be while also, as a game, creating incredibly potent alignment, expansion, and calibration.

Involve your loved ones - especially kids - and be ready, because giggles are about to become your new normal.

Align, Expand, and Calibrate - Your Stairway to Joy

 ay 24

ALIGNMENT in and with your positive mind is key to living a wonderful life, because what you think you will feel, and that mix together creates your next—which explains why you want to align with good feeling thoughts, even though lots of times it's easier to go for the negative since most of us are well trained in the downer-thought compartment.

But you actually have power! Your conscious focus can shift any thought to positive by choosing better beliefs more and more, programing you to automatically BE and live in a new high-for-life and better way!

How will you accomplish that? Is it by making a positive-thought list, finding the well-feeling opposite of every unwell thought, or by going with your gut that is saying, "What you just thought doesn't feel good, please choose better?"

_____
_____
_____
_____
_____
_____
_____
_____
_____
_____
_____
_____

Align, Expand, and Calibrate - Your Stairway to Joy

 ay 25

ALIGNING with good feelings that help you to enjoy life is a choice—maybe not one that feels natural, but one that can be learned.

Focus like a hawk on your feelings. Notice when you don't feel good, and do something about it—best to do so with urgency! How will you make sure that you will give all your might?

Align, Expand, and Calibrate - Your Stairway to Joy

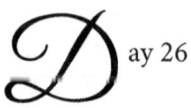

Day 26

EXPANDING in all well-feelings is a natural remedy for longevity—turning up your joy and vividness and re-setting every cell of your whole being towards healing, success, and abundance, which is in direct alignment with your inner soul-you. So instead of being happy and immediately brushing it off to go on to the next adventure, pause when you feel phenomenal and breathe into expanding yourself wide and big in that beautiful essence—the same way you spread yourself wide on your comfy sofa. Go overboard here, remember; it's a winning thing to do!

Align, Expand, and Calibrate - Your Stairway to Joy

# Day 27

CALIBRATING IS an action that can be done on many levels. Energetically, it means that you are right there side-by-side with your ever-calibrated soul being. Why? Because your inner being is always in THE capacity of height at any given moment, one that - of course - always changes and shifts. How will you stay on top of this energetically exhilarating way of living? Be ready, tomorrow we talk physical calibration!

Align, Expand, and Calibrate - Your Stairway to Joy

 ay 28

CALIBRATING on your physical level means that you live life vividly with your physical body—of course, to whatever extent is healthy and enjoyable for you. Why? When you are physically strong, you naturally feel powerful and that is in direct alignment with your impressive inner being—and expanding as such is invaluable. Are you pushing yourself to a good limit, or could you go a bit further with your physical body? What's possible for you?

_____
_____
_____
_____
_____
_____
_____
_____
_____
_____
_____
_____
_____
_____
_____
_____
_____
_____

Align, Expand, and Calibrate - Your Stairway to Joy

 ay 29

CALIBRATING the *action of thinking* into the frequency of a winner mind is...

You guessed it, thrillingly successful!

What calibrated thoughts can you come up with? Which ones will you choose to think all the time and pick over all else, to guarantee limitless enjoyment in your day-to-day moments?

_____
_____
_____
_____
_____
_____
_____
_____
_____
_____
_____
_____
_____
_____
_____
_____
_____
_____
_____
_____

Align, Expand, and Calibrate - Your Stairway to Joy

 ay 30

CAN you align with joy today, tomorrow, and ever after? Can you expand in the essence of bliss right now? Can you calibrate to BE and live as the biggest most powerful happiness—and is *pronto* possible? Great, so get on it! Now, even better—can you make this way of being and living your normal everyday style?

_____

Align, Expand, and Calibrate - Your Stairway to Joy

* * *

READY TO CONTINUE on your self-growth path? Get the next journal in this series: **Magick and Broomsticks - The Portal to Your Wild Side**

BONUS

Because hey, no one ever wants the goodness to end.

Align, expand, and calibrate more and more— and onward you go!

 ay 31

How many times will you infuse your personality, words, actions, and thoughts with your alignment, expansion, and calibration today? Or, at least, maybe I can get a potent "I'm giving my best to BE and live true to myself as much as possible!"

How committed are you—and can you commit even more?

Align, Expand, and Calibrate - Your Stairway to Joy

 ay 32

BECOMING ONE with consciousness means that you become nothing—so you can BE nothing, think nothing, feel nothing, expect nothing, and do nothing in the space of this beautiful nothingness.

Try it! Close your eyes and lay your body flat—breathe yourself into being ONE with that pure and limitless emptiness that you are at your core. There, a deep relaxation can set in and everything you always wanted, asked about, came here to experience, and way more has a chance to BE because as and in that nothingness - which is actually an everythingness - you are stepping out of your own way and give the OK to openly allow and receive the unknown. How does that feel?

_____
_____
_____
_____
_____
_____
_____
_____
_____
_____
_____
_____
_____
_____
_____
_____
_____

Align, Expand, and Calibrate - Your Stairway to Joy

ay 33

BEING RADIANT, magnetized, vitalized, full of yourself, and in complete love with yourself - as well as thinking the highest of yourself - is healthy! It's called alignment, expansion, and calibration—it's your birthright to BE and live. What are you waiting for?

Align, Expand, and Calibrate - Your Stairway to Joy

 ay 34

TAKE your sweet time and practice becoming a genius *aligner*, *expander*, and *calibrater*! But beware, I did not say "stick your head into the sand until better times arrive." NOW is the only time that you have, so go for it spectacular *journaler*, you have my support—besides, you so got this!

___
___
___
___
___
___
___
___
___
___
___
___
___
___
___
___
___
___
___
___
___
___

Align, Expand, and Calibrate - Your Stairway to Joy

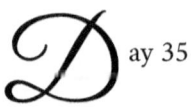 ay 35

NAY-SAYERS, negative-ers, and down-ers are aligned, just not with what you are seeking to align with. Does that make it wrong? No! It just isn't what you want; hence, you are working with this journal. So with an I-dont-care-ness and I-let-them-be-ness, turn your head towards your heart to focus on your courtship with yourself—in which you love yourself enough to create alignment, expansion, and calibration as YOU.

Oh my, you are glowing! Must be your alignment!

Align, Expand, and Calibrate - Your Stairway to Joy

AND NOW IT'S YOUR TURN!

The following are your magical pages to align, expand, and calibrate in secret!

BE 100% true to yourself here!

 ay 36

I ALIGN, expand, and calibrate because…

___

Align, Expand, and Calibrate - Your Stairway to Joy

 Day 37

ALIGNMENT, expansion, and calibration gives me...

_____
_____
_____
_____
_____
_____
_____
_____
_____
_____
_____
_____
_____
_____
_____
_____
_____
_____
_____
_____
_____

Align, Expand, and Calibrate - Your Stairway to Joy

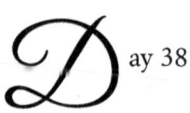ay 38

ALIGNING, expanding, and calibrating makes me…

Align, Expand, and Calibrate - Your Stairway to Joy

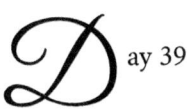Day 39

ALIGNMENT, expansion, and calibration creates...

Align, Expand, and Calibrate - Your Stairway to Joy

 ay 40

TO ALIGN, expand, and calibrate is a creative lifestyle because…

___

Align, Expand, and Calibrate - Your Stairway to Joy

* * *

Don't forget to leave a review on Amazon.com and Goodreads.com as soon as you can, as your kind feedback helps other readers find my books easier. Thank you!

ALSO BY JACQUELINE PIRTLE

365 Days of Happiness

Because happiness is a piece of cake!

This passage book invites you to create a daily habit to live your every day joy, and is the parent companion to *365 Days of Happiness*, the journal workbook.

* * *

365 Days of Happiness - Special Edition

Because happiness is a piece of cake

This beautiful Special Edition of the bestseller *365 Days of Happiness: Because happiness is a piece of cake* has room for your notes after every daily passage.

* * *

365 Days of Happiness - Journal Workbook

Because happiness is a piece of cake

This enlightening journal workbook is your daily tool to create a habit of living your every day bliss, and is the companion to *365 Days of Happiness: Because happiness is a piece of cake.*

* * *

Life IS Beautiful - Here's to New Beginnings

If you like digging deeper into the meaning of life and are inspired by spirituality, then you'll love Jacqueline's effective teachings.

* * *

Parenting Through the Eyes of Lollipops
A Guide to Conscious Parenting

If you like harmony at home and laughter in the house, then you'll love Jacqueline's inspirational methods.

* * *

What it Means to BE a Woman
And Yes! Women do Poop!

If you like to live free, empowered, and want to decide for yourself, then you'll love Jacqueline's liberating ways.

* * *

Life-changing Journals

What. If. - Turning your IFs into it IS!

Open - Where it all starts!

To BE and Live - The reason you are here!

High for Life - The best case scenario!

Bragging - Because you're worth it!

Of Course - Because why wait...

Magick and Broomsticks - The Portal to Your Wild Side

Every journal comes in two lengths:

A 30 day journal

A 90 day journal - The Extended Edition

If you like being in charge of your own life, turning your dreams into reality, enjoy journaling, and want to squeeze the most out of your time, then you'll love Jacqueline's uplifting teachings.

ABOUT THE AUTHOR

Bestselling author, podcaster, and holistic practitioner, Jacqueline Pirtle, has twenty-four years of experience helping thousands of clients discover their own happiness. Jacqueline is the owner of **FreakyHealer** and has shared her solid teachings through her podcast *The Daily Freak*, sessions, workshops, presentations, and books with clients all over the world. She holds international degrees in holistic health and natural living. Her effective healing work has been featured in print and online magazines, podcasts, radio shows, on TV, and in the documentary *The Overly Emotional Child by Learning Success*, available on Amazon Prime.

For any questions you might have, to sign up for Jacqueline's newsletter, and for more information on whatever else she is up to, visit www.freakyhealer.com and her social media accounts @freakyhealer.

www.ingramcontent.com/pod-product-compliance
Lightning Source LLC
Chambersburg PA
CBHW071423070526
44578CB00003B/669